57 Famous Classical Pieces for Piano

Play Songs by the Greatest Classical Composers With Original Sheet Music and Medium-Level Pieces in Order Of Difficulty

SCAN HERE
TO GET THE EXTRA CONTENT

OR ACCESS THE FOLLOWING LINK:
https://urly.it/3ztqw

BIOGRAPHIES, STORIES, AND ACCOUNTS
of the composers and pieces featured in the book

1 Discover the Lives Behind the Notes: **Fascinating stories of legendary composers such as Mozart, Bach, Beethoven, Chopin**, and many others.

2 Exclusive Details: **Delve into the stories behind their timeless masterpieces and uncover the hidden secrets in composition.**

3 **Enrich Your Musical Experience:** In addition to knowledge, receive 57 classic piano pieces, carefully selected to enhance your journey in the world of music.

Foreword:

I always advise my students to **listen to the piece before reading and studying it,**

you only need to do a **YouTube search by typing in the title and composer** to find it easily.

I also suggest that you listen, if possible, to multiple pianists so that you are not influenced by a single performance

The collection is for educational purposes to help the young student/pianist:

In fact, **the pieces are in order of difficulty to make learning more gradual, easy and orderly.**

Fingerings, dynamics and articulation have been added to each piece (the revision of the pieces was done by Mauro Costa)

Inside the book you will find a collection of **original famous classical pieces, exactly as the composer conceived and wrote them**

Layout: Mauro Costa

© 2023 Mauro Costa/ www.ProtectMyWork.com

Independent Publication

INDEX

Album for the Young

Op. 68, n.3

Robert Alexander Schumann
(1810-1856)

Minuet in F Major K 2

Wolfgang Amadeus Mozart
(1756-1791)

Album for the Young

Op. 68, n.1

Robert Alexander Schumann
(1810-1856)

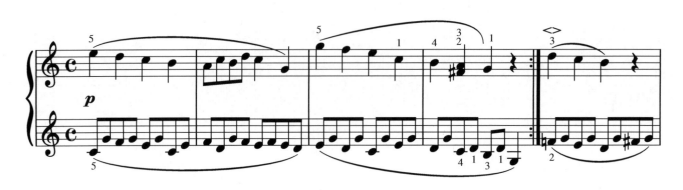

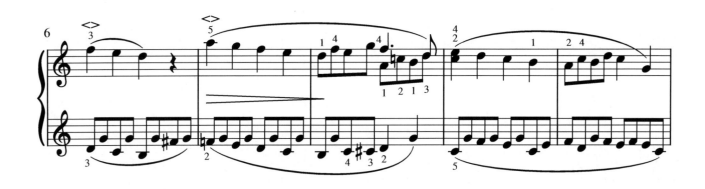

Minuet in G Major
BWV 114

J. S. Bach

Mnuet in G Major

K1 n. 1e

Wolfgang Amadeus Mozart
(1756 - 1791)

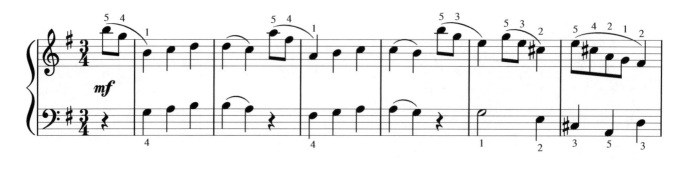

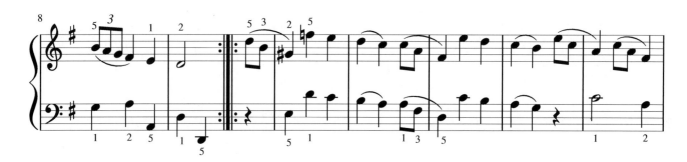

Trio

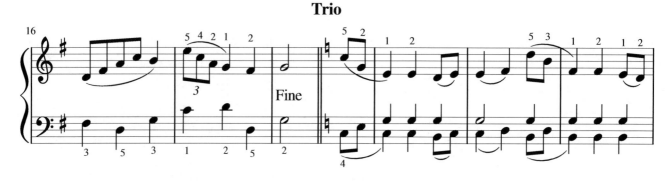

Minuetto da Capo al Fine

10

Album for the Young

Op.68 n.2

R.Schumann (1810-1856)

Vivo e deciso ♩ = 120

Minuet in G minor
BWV 115

J. S. Bach

Musette in D major
BWV 126

J. S. Bach

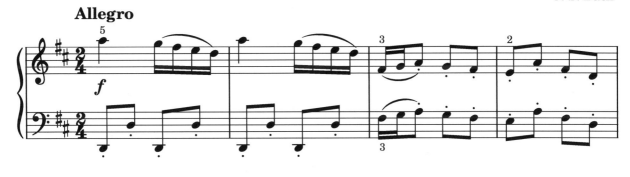

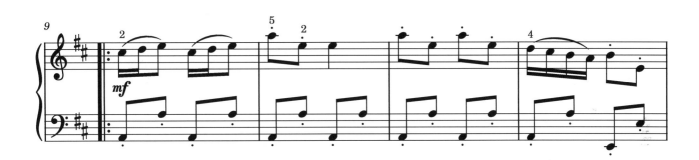

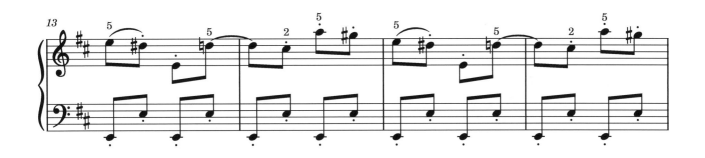

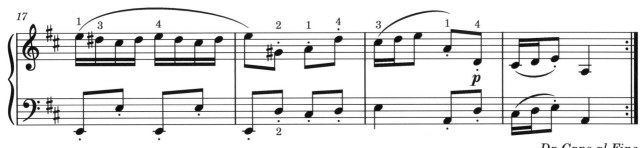

Da Capo al Fine

Allegretto
Op.125 n.10

Anton Diabelli (1781-1858)

German Dance
WoO 13 n. 9

L. van Beethoven

Allegro

Piano Sonatina Op. 151 No. 1

2nd movement

Anton Diabelli (1781-1858)

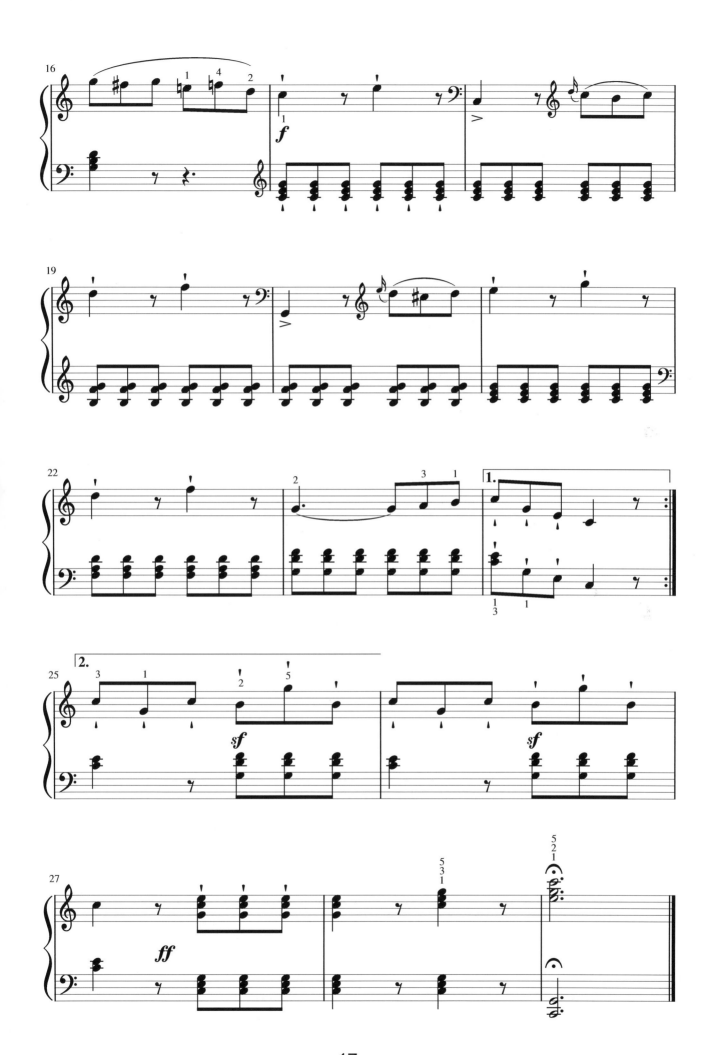

Wiosna "Spring"

Op. 74 No. 2

Fryderyk Franciszek Chopin
(1810–1849)

19

Sonatina in C Major
Op. 36 n. 1

M. Clementi

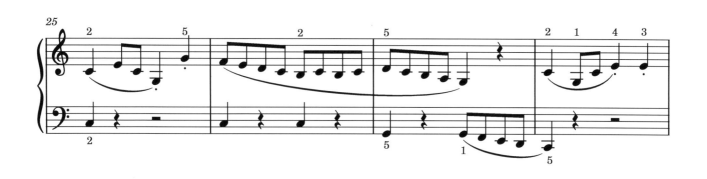

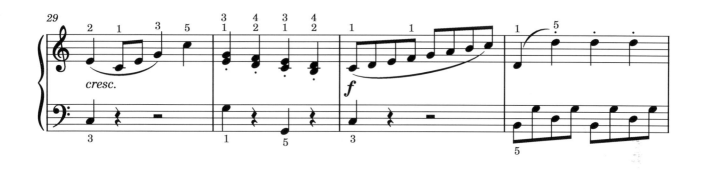

21

Prelude in C Major
BWV 846

J. S. Bach

Moderato

continua legato

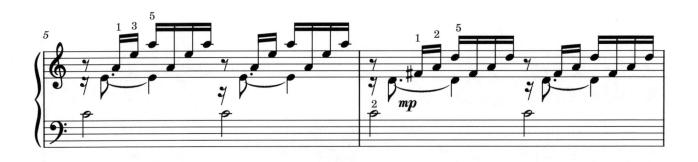

23

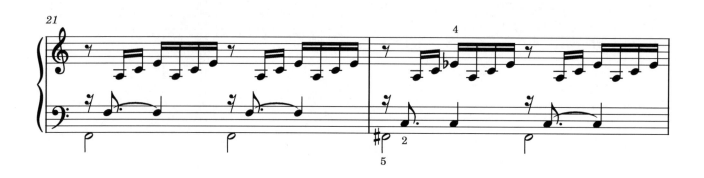

Old French Song

Op. 39, n. 16

Pyotr Ilyich Tchaikovsky
(1840 - 1893)

Moderato

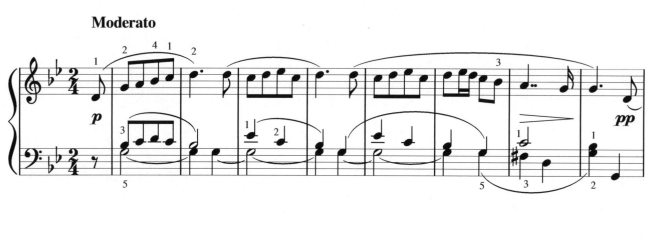

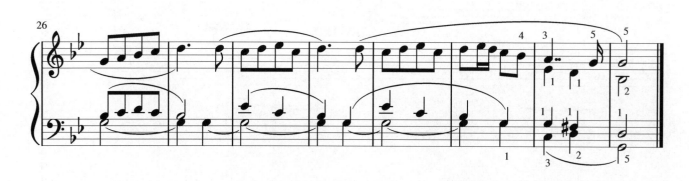

Album for the Young

Op. 68, n.7

Robert Alexander Schumann
(1810-1856)

Album for the Young

Op. 68, n.10

Robert Alexander Schumann
(1810-1856)

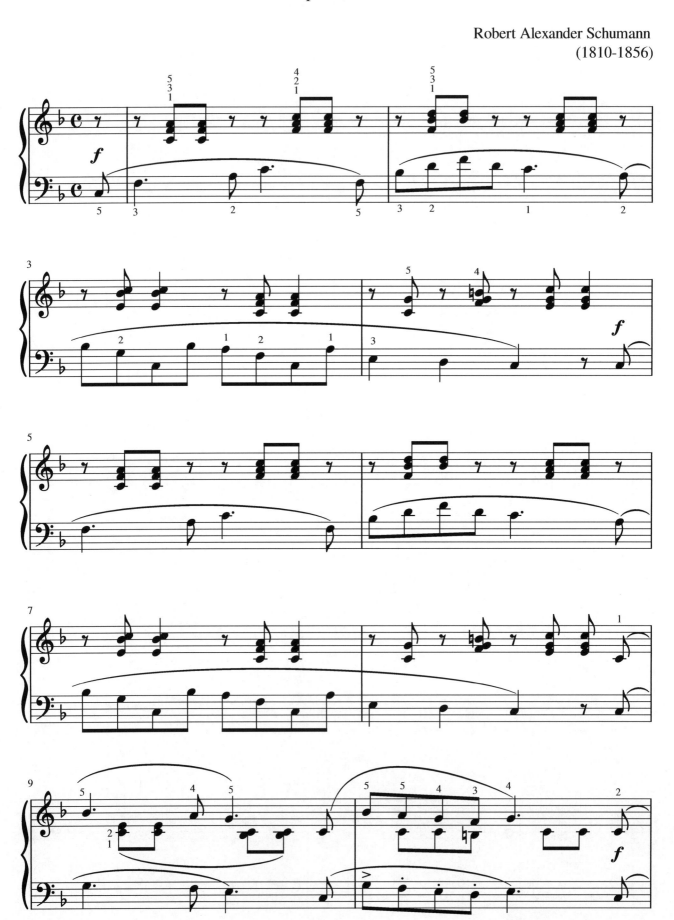

29

The New Doll

Op. 39, n. 9

Pyotr Ilyich Tchaikovsky
(1840 - 1893)

31

Arabesque
Op. 100 n. 2

J. F. F. Burgmüller

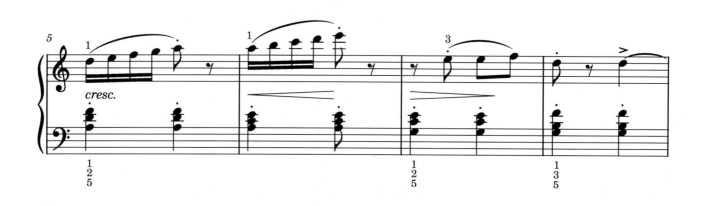

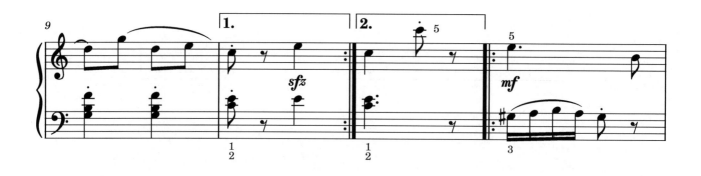

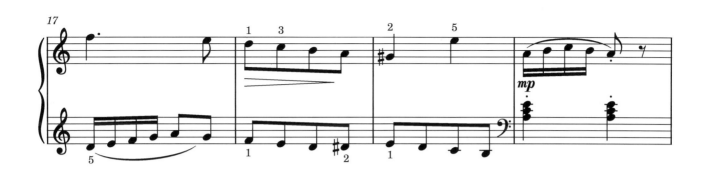

Album for the Young

Op. 68, n.8

Robert Alexander Schumann
(1810-1856)

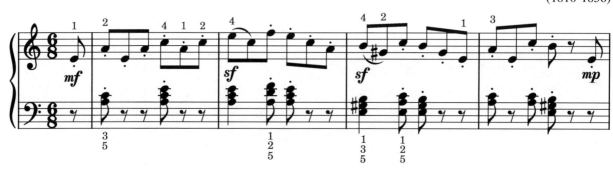

Etude "Ballade"
Op. 100 n. 15

F. Burgmüller

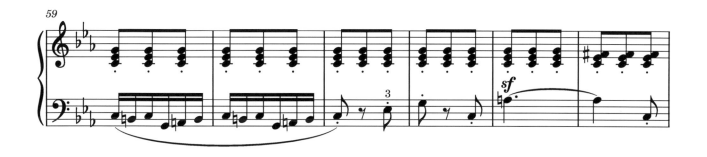

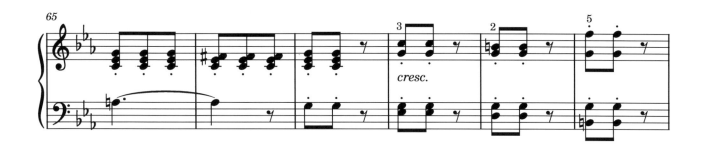

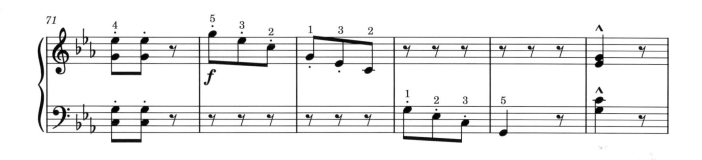

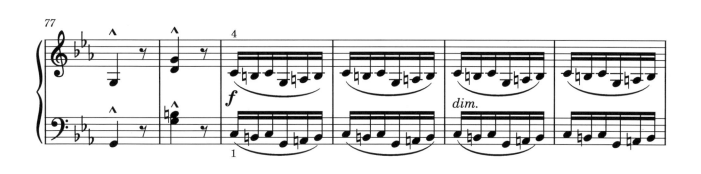

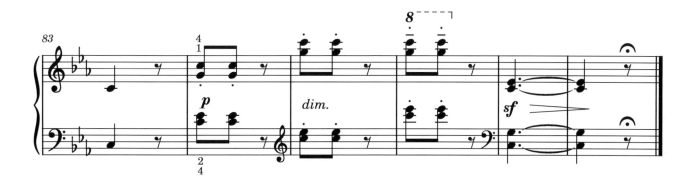

Gymnopédie n. 1

E. Satie

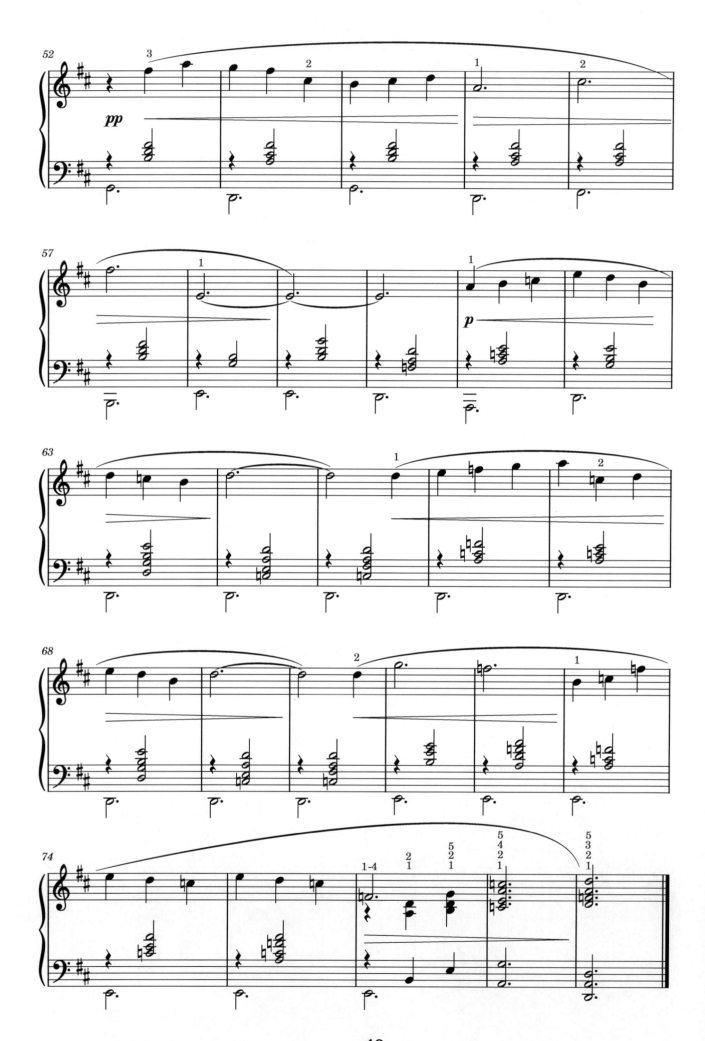

40

Tarantella

Op. 100 n. 20

J. F. Burgmüller

43

Spinning Song
Op. 14, No. 4

Albert Ellmenreich
(1816-1905)

45

Prelude in C Minor

Op. 28 No. 20

Fryderyk Franciszek Chopin
(1810–1849)

Harmony of the Angels

Op. 100, No. 21

Friedrich Burgmüller
(1806-1874)

49

Prelude in E Minor

Op. 28 No. 4

Fryderyk Franciszek Chopin
(1810–1849)

51

Prelude in B Minor

Op.28 n.6

Fryderyk Franciszek Chopin
(1810–1849)

Arietta

Op.12 n.1

Edvard Grieg (1843-1907)

Poco Andante e sostenuto

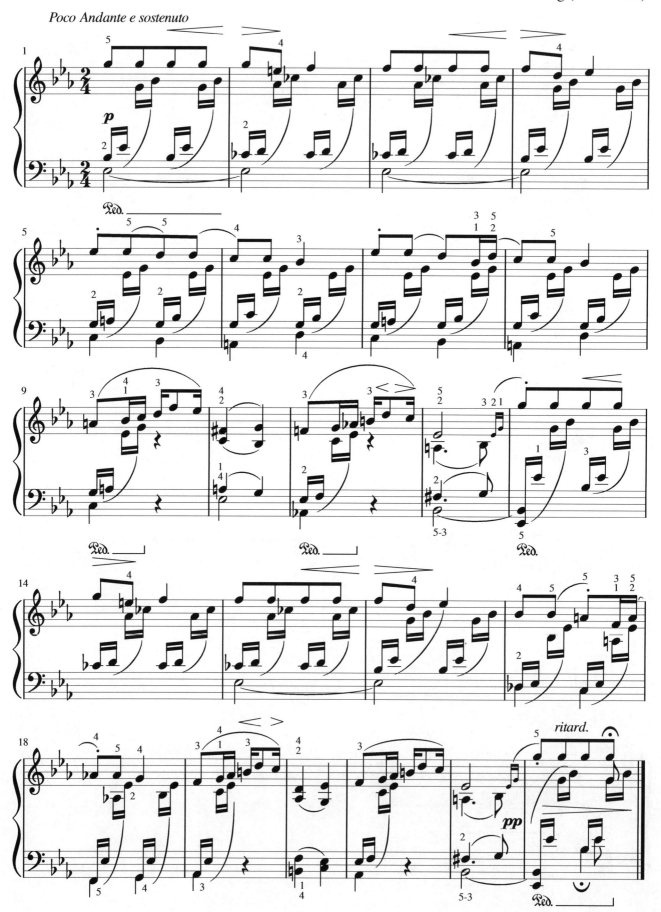

Piano Sonatina Op. 55 No. 1

1st movement

Friedrich Kuhlau (1786-1832)

Piano Sonatina op 36 no 2

1st movement

Muzio Clementi (1752-1832)

59

Minuet in C Minor

Franz Joseph Haydn
(1732-1809)

Allegro in F Major

Franz Joseph Haydn
(1732-1809)

63

To a Wild Rose
Op. 51 n. 1

E. MacDowell

65

Piano Sonatina Op. 36 No. 2

3rd movement

Muzio Clementi (1752-1832)

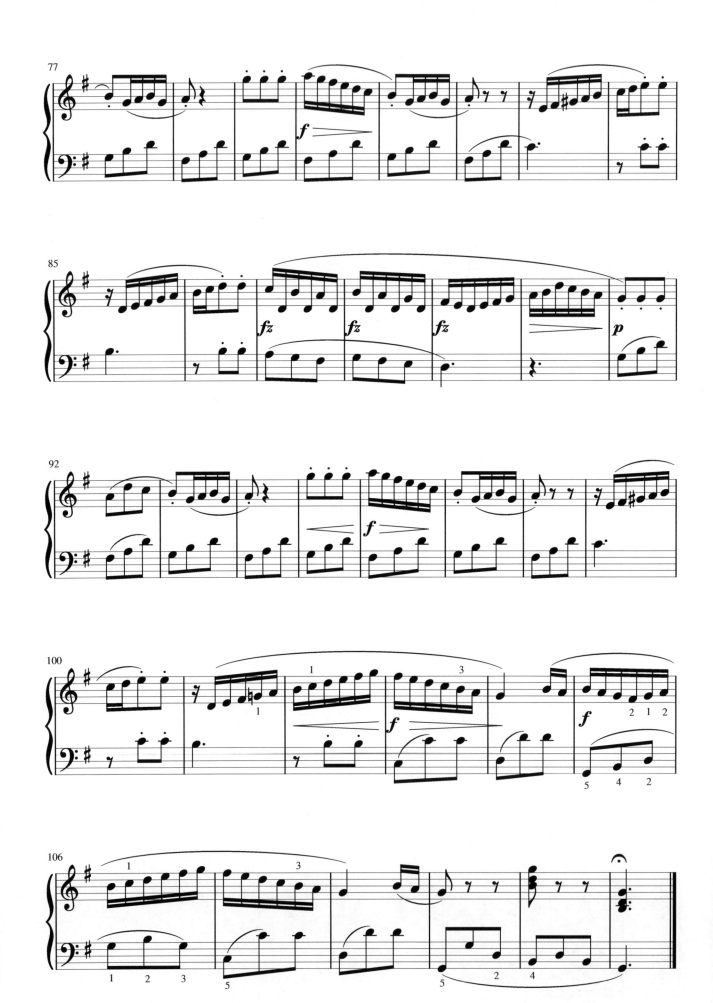

68

Etude "L' Orage"
Op.109 No. 13

Friedrich Burgmüller
(1806-1874)

70

71

Piano Sonatina Op. 36 No. 3
1st movement

Muzio Clementi (1752-1832)

75

Etudes "Alla Tarantella"
Op.39 n.2

Edward Alexander MacDowell
(1860-1908))

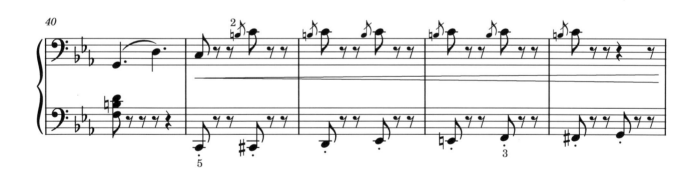

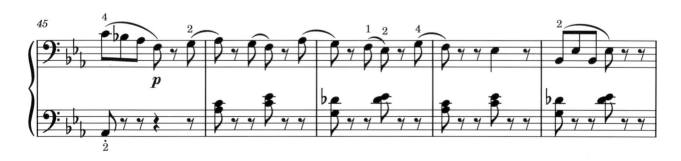

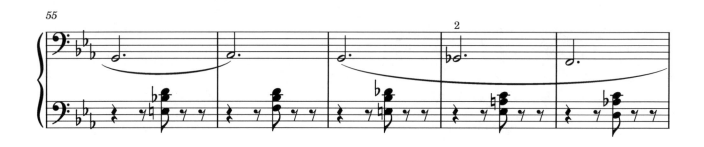

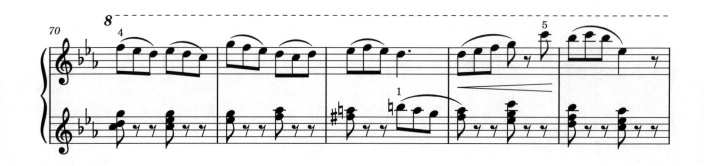

78

Praeambulum Supra Jesu, Meine Freude

KWV 502

J. L. Krebs

81

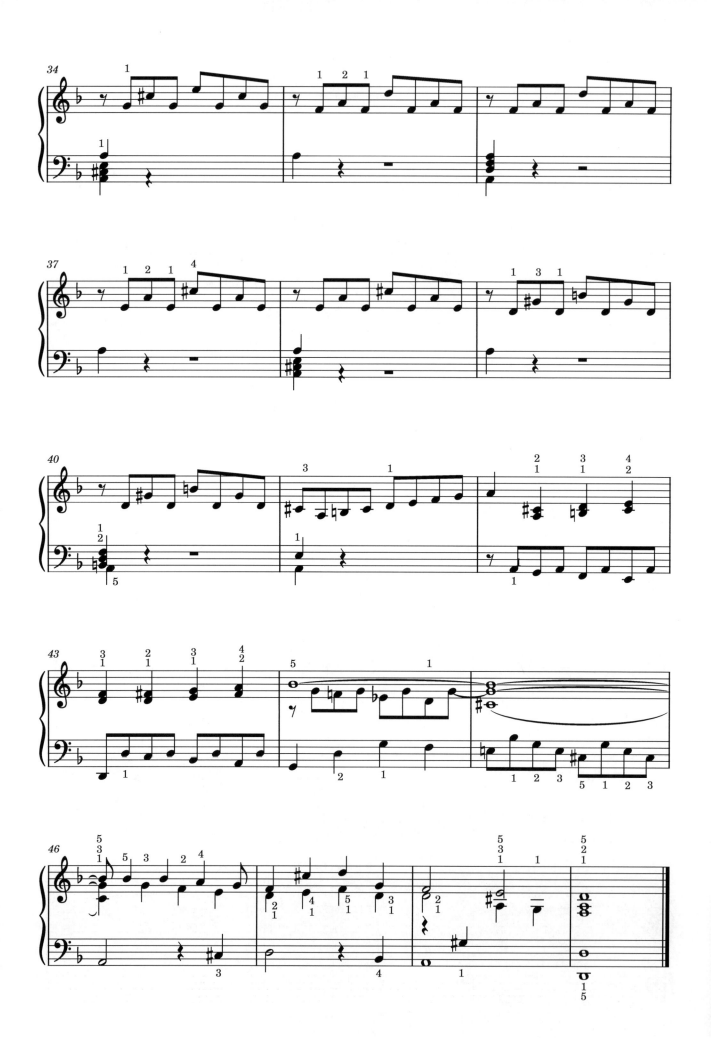

Etude in D Major
Op.46 No.8

Stephen Heller
(1813–1888)

Andante cantabile

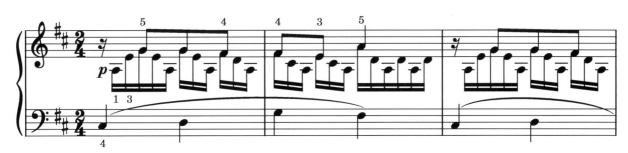

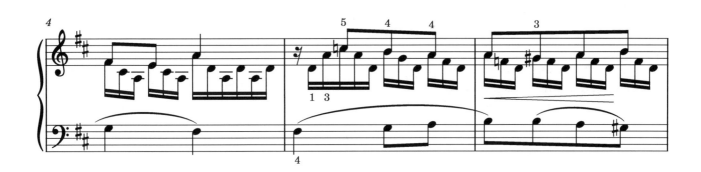

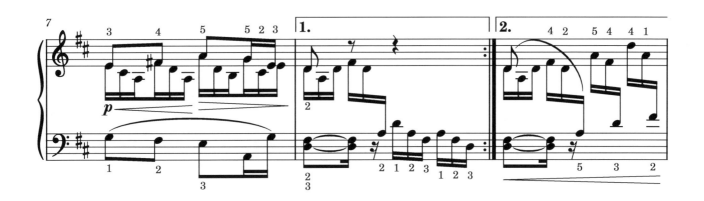

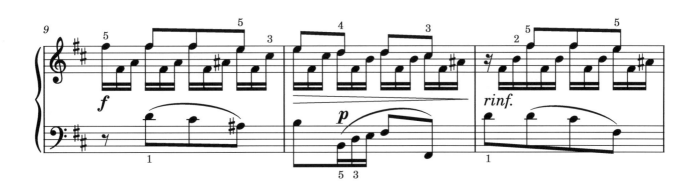

85

"Raindrop" Prelude

Op. 28 n. 15

Fryderyk Franciszek Chopin
(1810–1849)

87

Piano Sonata No. 16 in C Major

K. 545   2nd movement

Wolfgang Amadeus Mozart
(1756 - 1791)

Andante

93

95

Valzer

Op. 12, No. 2

Edvard Grieg (1843-1907)

Elfin Dance

Op 12, No. 4

Edvard Grieg (1843-1907)

Songs Without Words

Op. 19 n. 6

Felix Mendelssohn Bartholdy
(1809-1847)

Waltz
Op.38 n.7

Edvard Grieg (1843-1907)

Piano Sonata "Moonlight"

Op. 27 No. 2

Ludwig van Beethoven
(1770–1827)

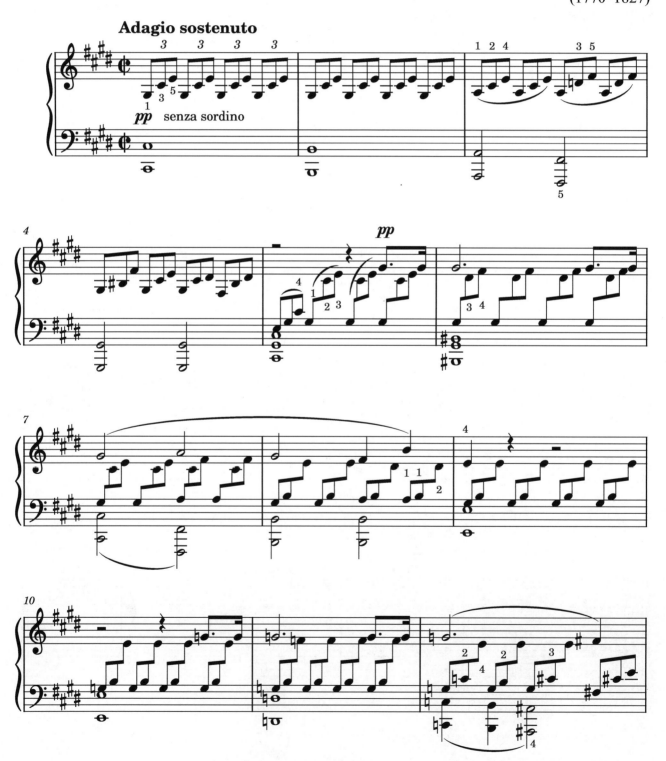

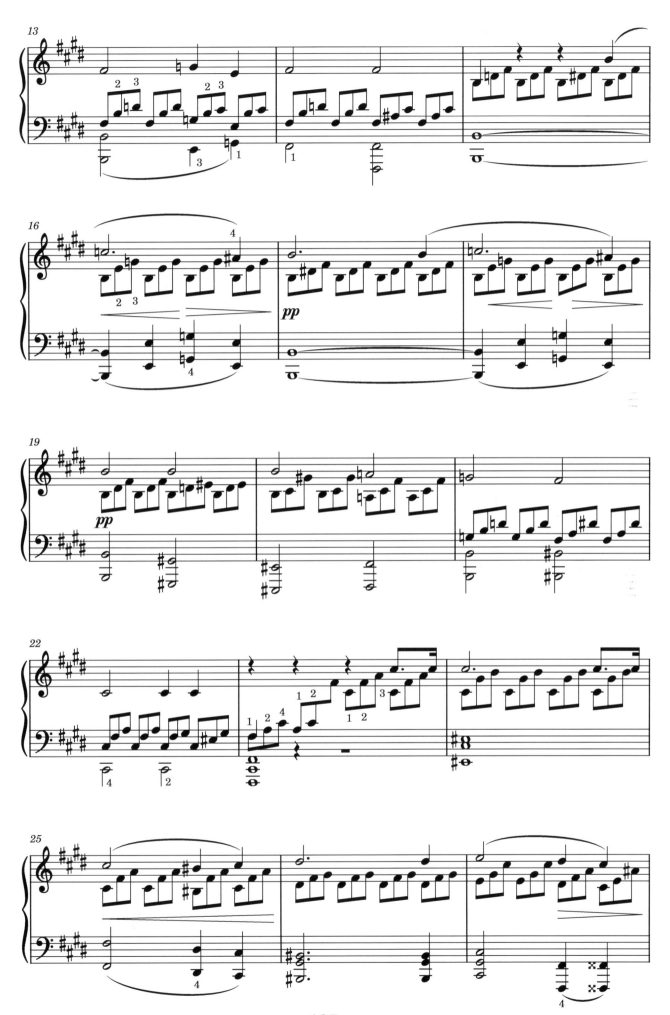

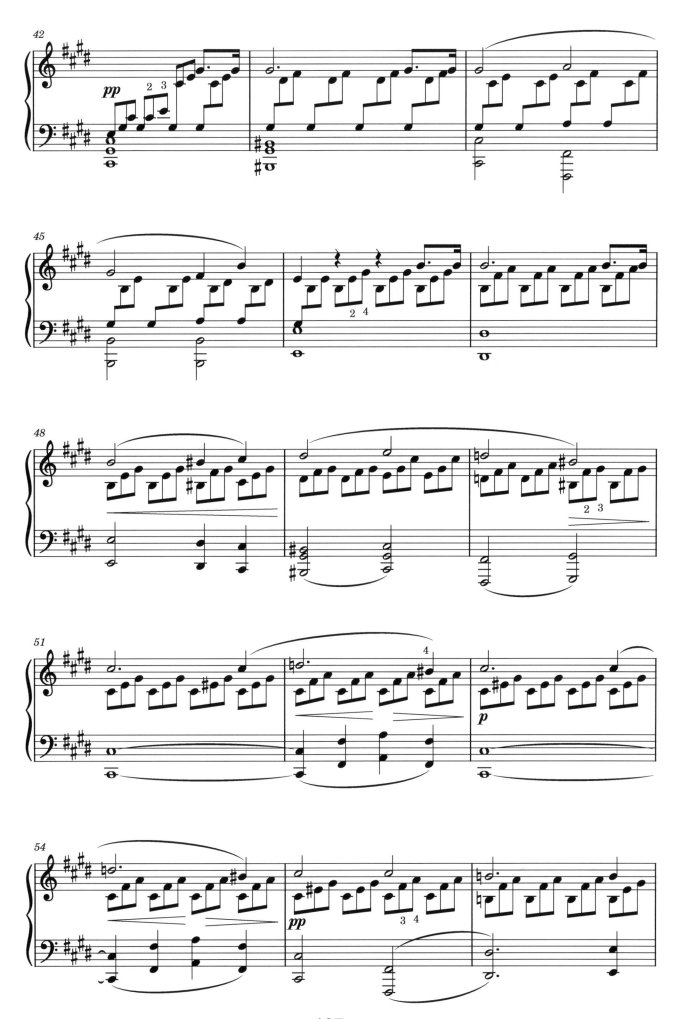

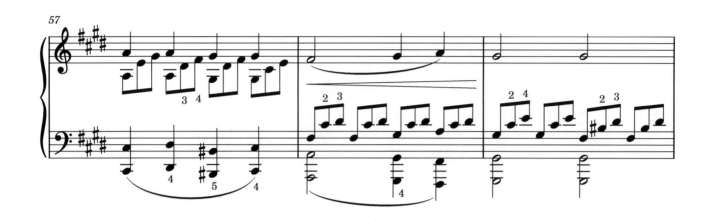

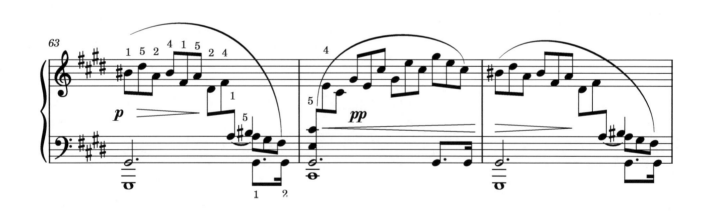

Prelude in D minor

BWV 851

J.S.Bach (1685-1750)

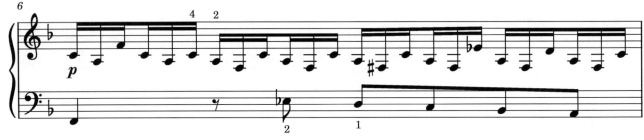

111

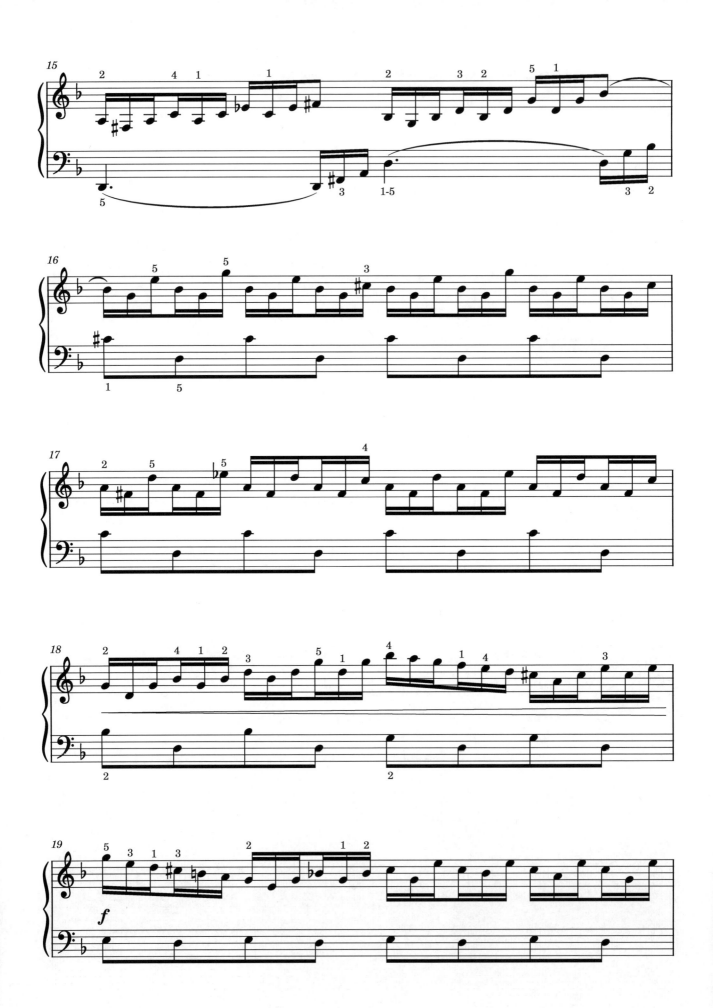

Waltz in B Minor

Op.69 n.2

Fryderyk Franciszek Chopin
(1810 - 1849)

115

116

118

Waltz in A ♭ Major

Opus 69 No. 1

Frédéric François Chopin
(1810 - 1849)

Prelude in C minor

BWV 847

J. S. Bach

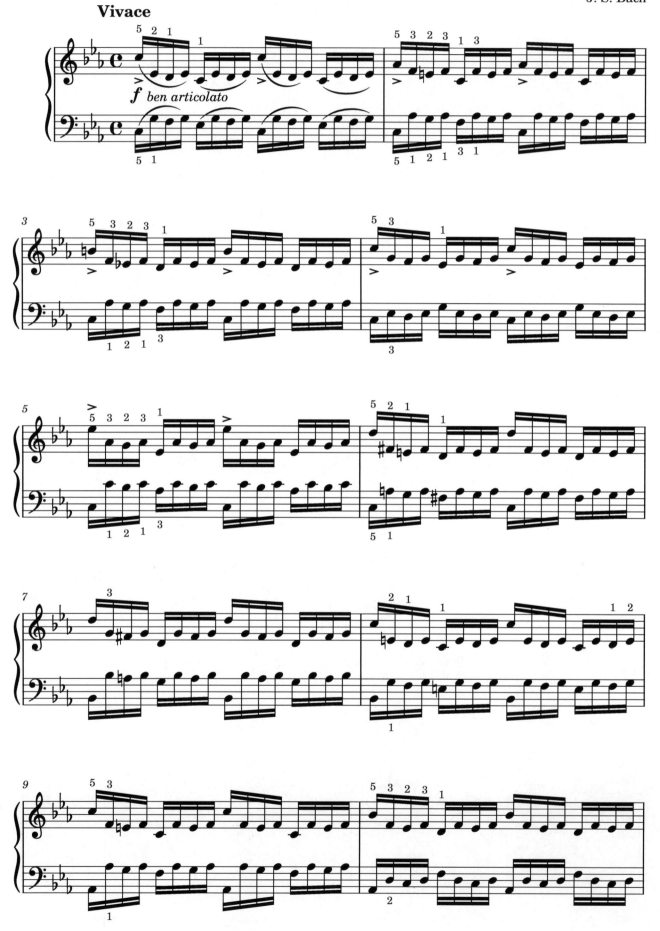

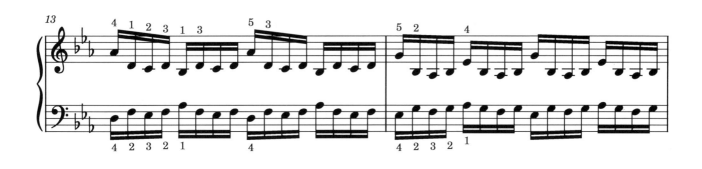

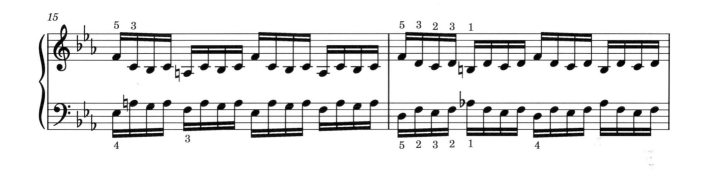

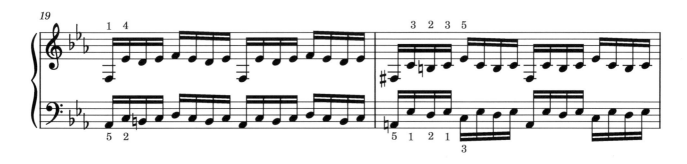

125

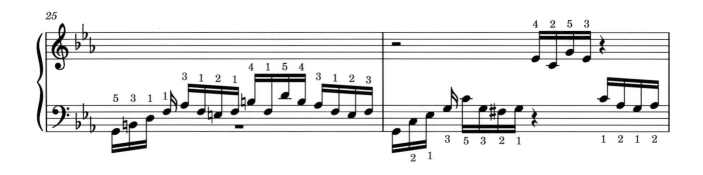

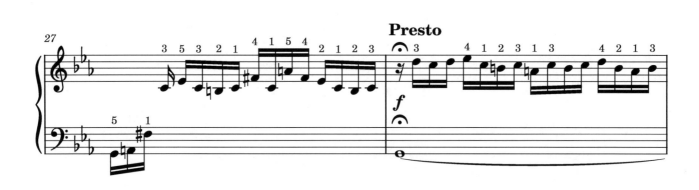

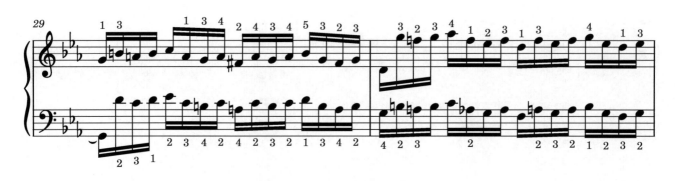

126

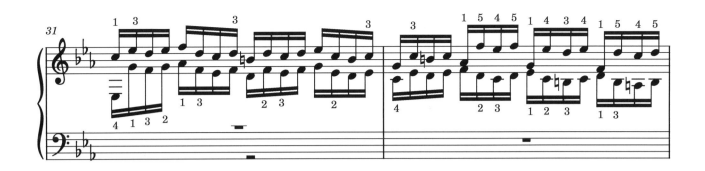

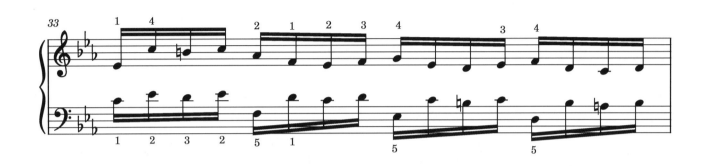

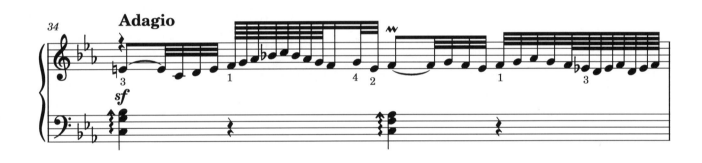

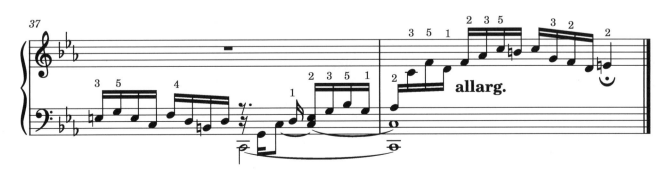

La Fille Aux Cheveux De Lin

C. Debussy

Molto calmo ed espressivo

Piano Sonata No. 16 in C Major, K. 545

1st movement

Wolfgang Amadeus Mozart
(1756–1791)

Sonata in D minor K.1

Domenico Scarlatti
(1685-1757)

Piano Sonata No. 8

2nd Movement

Ludwig van Beethoven
(1770 - 1827)

139

140

143

Für Elise
WoO 59

L.V. Beethoven(1770-1827)

144

145

Piano Sonata No. 11 in A Major
K. 331   Alla Turca

Wolfgang Amadeus Mozart
(1756–1791)

Allegretto

150

Made in the USA
Las Vegas, NV
06 December 2024

13436480R00085